Usborne Naturetrail
Birdwatching

Usborne Naturetrail
Insects
& other creepy-crawlies

Damselfly
Cricket
Bumble bee
Great-diving beetle
Common blue butterfly

Usborne Naturetrail
Rocks & Fossils

Amb...
Amet...
Red...
Amm...
Nat...

Herring gull
Gannet

Usborne Naturetrail
Seashore

Yellow horned poppy
Edible crab
Carhoning wrack
Gut Laver
Bladder wrack

Usborne Naturetrail
Trees

Rowan ber...
Wych elm fruits
Peach
Sycamore fruit
Cross-section of a tree trunk

Pressing flowers

Usborne Naturetrail
Wild Flowers

Poppy plant
Poppy flower
Seeds
Poppy fruit

Usborne Naturetrail
Seashore

Usborne Naturetrail
Seashore

Sarah Courtauld and Conrad Mason

Designed by Kate Rimmer

Illustrated by
Brin Edwards and Non Figg

Edited by Jane Chisholm

Consultants: Dr Mandy Holloway,
Natural History Museum, and Derek Niemann,
Royal Society for the Protection of Birds

Internet links

The Usborne Quicklinks Website is packed with thousands of links to all the best websites on the internet. The websites include information, video clips, sounds, games and animations that support and enhance the information in Usborne Internet-linked books.

To visit the recommended websites for **Naturetrail Seashore**, go to the Usborne Quicklinks Website at **www.usborne-quicklinks.com** and enter the keywords: **naturetrail seashore**.

When using the internet please follow the internet safety guidelines displayed on the Usborne Quicklinks Website. The recommended websites in Usborne Quicklinks are regularly reviewed and updated, but Usborne Publishing Ltd is not responsible for the content or availability of any website other than its own. We recommend that children are supervised while using the internet.

CONTENTS

Exploring the seashore

Rocky shores

Sandy shores

Shells

Birds

In the sea

Near the shore

Exploring the seashore

When you look at a seashore, it might seem empty, but in fact it is full of hidden life. If you dig in the sand, turn over a pebble or peer into a rock pool, you can discover lots of fascinating animals and plants.

With the roaring wind, pounding waves and predators from land and sea, the seashore is a tough place to survive. The animals that live there have adapted to become some of the most bizarre and intriguing creatures on the planet.

Kittiwakes are gulls that nest in cracks in cliffs.

Life on the shore

Where an animal lives is called its habitat. There are lots of different ones to discover at the shore: rock pools, muddy shores, sandy beaches and sea cliffs. Each habitat attracts different kinds of wildlife. You might see butterflies flitting through a sand dune, but if you peer into a rock pool you could spot bright orange starfish and spiny animals called sea urchins.

A beach will contain more than one type of habitat: it might have rocks at one end, and sand dunes at the other. And one habitat oftens blends into another. So you'll find some overlap between the different habitats and the creatures that live there.

These spiky animals are called sea urchins.

Turnstones are birds that flip over pebbles to find food.

Starfish

This crab lives inside a shell.

Seashore surprises

Many seashore creatures aren't quite what they seem. Sea anemones, for example, look like small plants, but they're actually dangerous animals with poisonous tentacles. A razor shell might not look like a fast moving animal, but if you go near it, it will disappear into the sand in a flash. And sea cucumbers might look like vegetables – but they're actually underwater animals that will squirt their sticky guts over an attacker.

SHORE WARS

When attacked, a sea cucumber shoots out sticky threads.

This anemone has tentacles which it can use to paralyse its prey.

A sea bird called a cormorant dives to catch a fish.

Sanderling

Razor shell

Moon jellyfish

Common blue butterfly

Barnacles are tiny animals that glue themselves to rocks.

Edible crab

Common bindweed

Trailing plant with thick, shiny leaves. Found on sand dunes and sometimes on shingle. Flowers June-Sept.

*Your field guide will tell you what times of year to look out for different species.

Photo of starfish page in field guide

Using a field guide

When you visit a seashore, there will probably be some animals and plants that you recognize. But if you find something you can't identify, you'll need to use a field guide. Just follow the steps below:

1. Look closely at your find and note down as many details as you can.

Purply red colour

Tiny spines

Thirteen arms

2. Flick through your field guide until you've found a section with the plants or animals that look most like your find.

3. See if any of the pictures matches what you can see.

There are lots of starfish here, but only one with white spines and more than 10 arms...

Sea Urchins and Starfish

These animals have prickly spines on their skin and rows of suckers which they use to pull themselves along and to hold onto rocks.

Brown serpent-star
Stripes on arms darken with age. Mediterranean. 10-15cm.

Common mediterranean sea urchin
Holds bits of seaweed or shell over itself. Not in Britain. Up to 10cm.

Black sea urchin
Black spines. Lower shore and deep water. Not in Britain. 6-10cm.

Small purple-tipped sea urchin
Spines have purple tips. Under rocks and stones on lower shore. Up to 4cm.

Live sea urchin   Test

Edible sea urchin
On rocky shores and offshore but becoming rare. Spines drop off when sea urchin dies. Shell is called a test. Up to 15cm.

Sea potato
Sea urchin which lives in sand at low tide level. Leaves a dent on surface where it has burrowed. Empty shells, called tests, may be washed ashore in storms. 5-6cm long.

Common starfish
Five arms, like most starfish. Tips often turn up when starfish moves. Up to 50cm but those on shore only 5-10cm.

Mediterranean multi-armed starfish
Six to eight arms, often of different lengths. 8-12cm.

Cushion starlet
Very small with short arms. Under rocks and in shady parts of rock pools. 1-2cm.

Spiny starfish
Large spines. Colour varies. On lower shore and in deep water. 8-12cm.

Small brittle star
Very common but hard to spot. Under stones. 3cm.

Small brittle star

Common brittle star
Very fragile, so handle gently. Under stones. 3-8cm.

Common brittle star

Sunstar
Preys on other starfish. Spiny, with up to 15 arms. Often beautifully patterned. 4-8cm.

43

Measuring your finds

Field guides will tell you the size of each creature, but some are measured differently from others. For example, jellyfish are measured without their tentacles, birds are measured from head to tail, and crabs are measured without their claws.

You can use this ruler to measure seashore creatures ➤

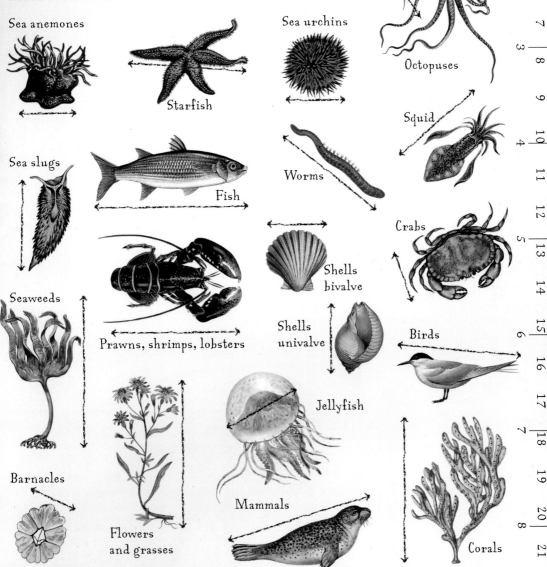

Sea anemones

Starfish

Sea urchins

Octopuses

Squid

Sea slugs

Fish

Worms

Crabs

Seaweeds

Prawns, shrimps, lobsters

Shells bivalve

Shells univalve

Birds

Barnacles

Flowers and grasses

Jellyfish

Mammals

Corals

cm 1 2 3 4 5 6 7 8 9 10 11 12 13 14 15 16 17 18 19 20 21 22

1 inch 2 3 4 5 6 7 8 9

11

Use a magnifying glass to look at fine details.

You can pop animals, such as crabs, inside a clear plastic tank full of water.

A long stick can be very useful to turn over seaweed.

Use a torch to peer into dark crevices in rocks.

Use a spade or a trowel to dig for creatures in the sand.

You can find small animals in the sand with a sieve.

Re-sealable bags can be useful for putting shells in.

A field guide will help you identify different plants and animals.

Seashore detective

The seashore is a brilliant place to become a nature detective. With a few simple bits of equipment, you can lure animals out of their nooks and crannies and study them up close. Here are some handy tips to help your seashore investigations.

 You might want to look at animals in a a tank to get a closer look at them. A clear plastic food container works very well.

 Always put water in the tank with the animals. Now you can look at it close up.

 Keep your tank in a rock pool or in the shade to keep the animals cool.

✓ After you've looked at animals, always put them back where you found them.

An edible crab feeds on mussels in a rock pool.

12

Taking notes

A nature detective's most important tool is a notebook. You can use yours to record clues to help you identify a seashore creature. First note down its appearance, and then try and work out what it's doing. Is it alone or in a group? How does it move? Is it keeping cool in the shade or warming itself in the sun? The more notes you make, the easier it will be to find out what it is.

For more handy seashore equipment see:

p27 to make an underwater viewer

p43 to make a worm watcher

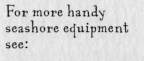

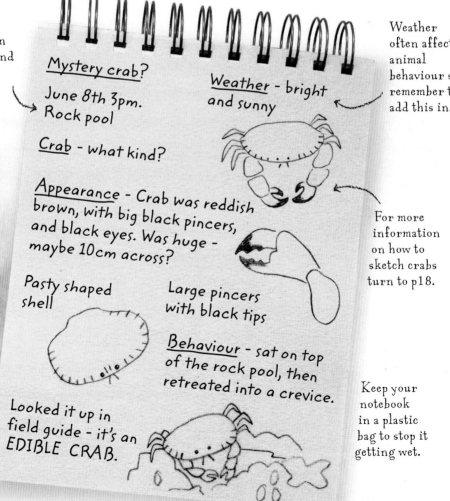

Note down the date and the time of day.

Weather often affects animal behaviour so remember to add this in.

Mystery crab?

June 8th 3pm. Rock pool

Weather - bright and sunny

Crab - what kind?

Appearance - Crab was reddish brown, with big black pincers, and black eyes. Was huge - maybe 10cm across?

For more information on how to sketch crabs turn to p18.

Pasty shaped shell

Large pincers with black tips

Behaviour - sat on top of the rock pool, then retreated into a crevice.

Keep your notebook in a plastic bag to stop it getting wet.

Looked it up in field guide - it's an EDIBLE CRAB.

TOP TIP

To get to know the different zones, explore a beach at low tide. Start at the sea and walk up towards the land. For every metre, write down what plants and animals you find. Do more animals live in some parts than in others? Can you spot the strandline?

Tides and zones

The sea creeps up and down the shore twice each day. This movement is known as the tide, and it affects everything that lives there. As the waves rush in, some plants are drenched by swirling water. Further up the beach, other plants just get a splash of salty spray. When the tide goes out, some animals in the sand start to dry up.

Scientists divide the beach into four main zones, according to how much time each zone spends getting wet each day.

Grasses

Splash zone

This is the highest part of the beach, which is never covered by the sea. The animals and plants are splashed by the salty waves when the tide comes in.

Upper zone

This zone can be uncovered for days. Animals that live here usually have shells to hide in for safety until the sea covers them again.

Channelled wrack

Rough periwinkles

Lichen

Strandline

This is the line at the top of the beach where the high tide deposits all sorts of objects from the sea.

Barnacles

How tides work

The Moon and the Sun have a powerful pull on the oceans. Imagine that they are strongmen, tugging the water in the oceans in different directions. As the position of the Moon, the Earth and the Sun changes, the oceans' water levels go up and down, creating the tides. When the Sun and Moon are line with each other, the tides are strongest (called spring tides). When the Sun and Moon pull in opposite ways, the tides are weaker (called neap tides).

Neap tide

The Sun and Moon pull in different directions, making weak tides.

Spring tide

The Sun and Moon pull in the same direction, making strong tides.

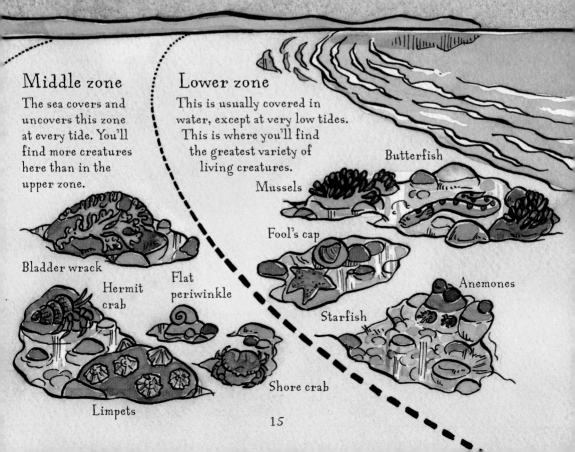

Middle zone
The sea covers and uncovers this zone at every tide. You'll find more creatures here than in the upper zone.

Lower zone
This is usually covered in water, except at very low tides. This is where you'll find the greatest variety of living creatures.

Butterfish

Mussels

Fool's cap

Bladder wrack

Hermit crab

Flat periwinkle

Anemones

Starfish

Shore crab

Limpets

15

Rabbits make longer tracks with their back paws than their front paws.

Front foot

Hind foot

You might spot fox tracks in sand dunes. They have four toes above a triangular pad.

Hind foot

Front foot

A seal has left these marks in the sand. You can see the flipper marks at each side.

Following tracks

Even if the shore looks deserted, you can identify lots of seashore creatures from the tracks they leave behind. Tracks show up well on soft, wet sand. If you can, look for them early in the morning, before they've been disturbed.

Reading the signs

Looking closely at tracks can give you clues about the animal that made them and what it was doing. If you spot some bird tracks in the sand, you could ask yourself a few simple questions. What direction was the bird going in? Can you tell what species it is? Follow the tracks and see where they lead you.

These tracks have three toes and webbing...

...Gulls have webbed feet...

...I followed the tracks and saw a herring gull flying off...

Webbing

Three toes

...so these tracks must belong to a herring gull.

Crabs leave these thick, wiggly tracks on the sand.

Making casts

You can start a collection of animal and bird footprints by making plaster casts of tracks. You'll need plaster of Paris, cardboard, some paperclips, a bowl, a spoon and a spade. When you've found a footprint, just follow the steps below:

1. Clip a piece of cardboard into a circle big enough to fit around the print.

2. Mix up the plaster of Paris in the bowl, according to the instructions on the packet. Pour it gently into the print. It should be about 2.5cm (1") deep.

3. Wash the spoon and bowl straight away. After about ten minutes, the plaster will harden. Then you can dig up the cast.

4. At home, remove the cardboard strips, and gently clean any sand or mud from the cast with a toothbrush.

5. If you paint the casts, you could make prints on paper like these.

PLANT RUBBING

You can use wax crayons to make rubbings of leaves or seaweed. You'll get the best results with plants that are hard, dry and fairly flat.

1. Place your plant on a piece of cardboard and cover it with a sheet of white paper.

2. Rub over the paper with a wax crayon, using even, parallel strokes.

3. You could copy the colours of the plant or experiment with your own colours.

Sketches and photos

One handy way to record seashore life is to make rough drawings. You don't have to be brilliant at drawing – quick sketches are easy to do and can help to identify different species. You can then add your notes around your drawing. Follow these steps to drawing different seashore creatures.

Crabs

1. Draw the body first

2. Then add in the pincers

3. Finally add the eyes and feelers

Birds

1. First draw an oval for the head, and a larger oval for the body

2. Add the eye, beak, legs, neck, feet and tail

3. Add in details of feathers

Flying birds   Starfish

Add wings to draw birds in flight

1. Start with the outline

2. Add the patterns and spikes

Taking photos

You can take great photos of wildlife with very basic equipment. Just remember these useful tips:

If possible, use a plain background - cluttered backgrounds can be distracting.

Don't get too close to an animal, or you may frighten it. Use a camera with a zoom if you have one.

Don't just take a portrait of an animal. Try to capture its behaviour as well.

Use a flash outdoors. On a cloudy day it can help brighten your photographs.

PLANT PRINT

You could take home dead seaweed or leaves to make a plant print. Just follow these simple steps:

1. Cover one side of your leaf with oil paint or shoe polish.

2. Place it on a piece of paper with the oily side downwards.

3. Cover it with another piece of paper and rub firmly over the paper.

4. Lift the paper and remove the leaf.

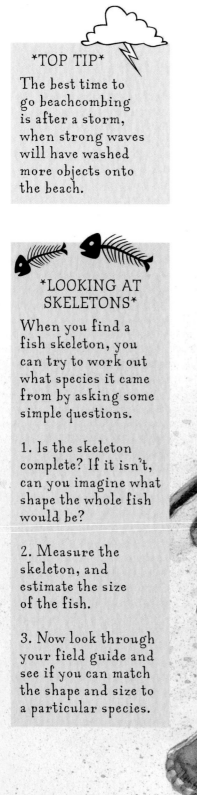

TOP TIP

The best time to go beachcombing is after a storm, when strong waves will have washed more objects onto the beach.

LOOKING AT SKELETONS

When you find a fish skeleton, you can try to work out what species it came from by asking some simple questions.

1. Is the skeleton complete? If it isn't, can you imagine what shape the whole fish would be?

2. Measure the skeleton, and estimate the size of the fish.

3. Now look through your field guide and see if you can match the shape and size to a particular species.

Beachcombing

Walking along the beach with your nose to the ground and seeing what you can find is called beachcombing. For a nature detective, there are lot of strange treasures to discover. Everything you pick up will have its own story to tell.

The best place to start searching is the strandline, where you can uncover all sorts of curious finds from jellyfish to 'mermaids' purses' – shiny capsules that are actually dogfish egg cases. Here are some of the objects you might find washed up on a beach.

Look out for jellyfish called Portuguese men-of-war. Don't touch them, as they can sting even when dead.

Mermaid's purse

Empty crab shells

Common jellyfish

Looking at driftwood

Even an ordinary looking piece of driftwood is fascinating if you look closely at it. You can often see where the water has etched away the softer parts of the wood and left the grain standing out.

If you find tiny holes (about 5mm across) in the wood, you'll know that gribbles have been there. These tiny animals eat their way into driftwood, lacing it with tunnels. Larger tunnels, which often have a chalky lining, are the work of shipworms. They use their two shells to drill their way into the wood.

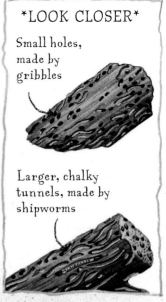

LOOK CLOSER

Small holes, made by gribbles

Larger, chalky tunnels, made by shipworms

These soft brown balls are the remains of a marine plant called Posidonia.

Driftwood

Although it looks like a bone, this is actually the shell of a squid-like creature called a cuttlefish.

This spongy ball is a whelk egg case.

These pieces of glass have been rubbed smooth by the waves.

Pebbles, riddled with worm tubes

Fish skeleton

This sea urchin's shell is still intact.

Making a nature diary

When you've got home from the seashore, you can put all your notes and sketches together to make a nature diary. It will be a record of your trip and it can also help you to understand more about the curious lives of seashore creatures.

If you return to the same seashore several times, you can build up a detailed account of the wildlife there.

Stick your prints and rubbings in

18th August   Sunny with clouds

Rock pool by edge of water

Walked across sand dune

Saw oystercatcher looking for food on the rocks

20th August   Cloudy

Rock pool by edge of water

Seaweed print

Seaweed rubbing

Saw bright anemone

Write up your observations

Stick photos and sketches into your diary

22

Secret lives

Perhaps the best thing about a wildlife diary is that it helps you to build up a picture of the lives of seashore plants and animals. For example, you could collect lots of notes about a particular animal. Then you'll begin to learn more about its life.

TOP TIP

Look up your local conservation society on the internet. Then you can send them reports of your wildlife sightings.

A mother seal with her pup

SEAL DIARY	
DATE	OBSERVATIONS
25th August	Saw twenty or so grey seals, basking on the sandbank in the morning sun.
2nd September	Several males have turned up. It's easy to tell which ones are the males - they are much bigger than the females, and have darker coats and huge noses.
5th September	Two baby seal pups have appeared, with thick white coats.
8th September	There are now 8 or so little pups. While we were watching, one of the adult seals waddled down to the water, hissing and barking.
21st September	Walked along the sandbank - but all the seals have gone. They must be out at sea.

Rocky shores

Peer into a rock pool and you can uncover
a magical underwater world of plants and
animals. You could see a tiny transparent
shrimp, darting backwards through the water,
a bristly starfish guzzling on a sea urchin, or the
claws of a crab poking out from under a stone.

The longer you look, the more you'll see, as
sea creatures rush out from hidden nooks and
crannies to hunt for food and see off intruders
– and then disappear into their hiding places.

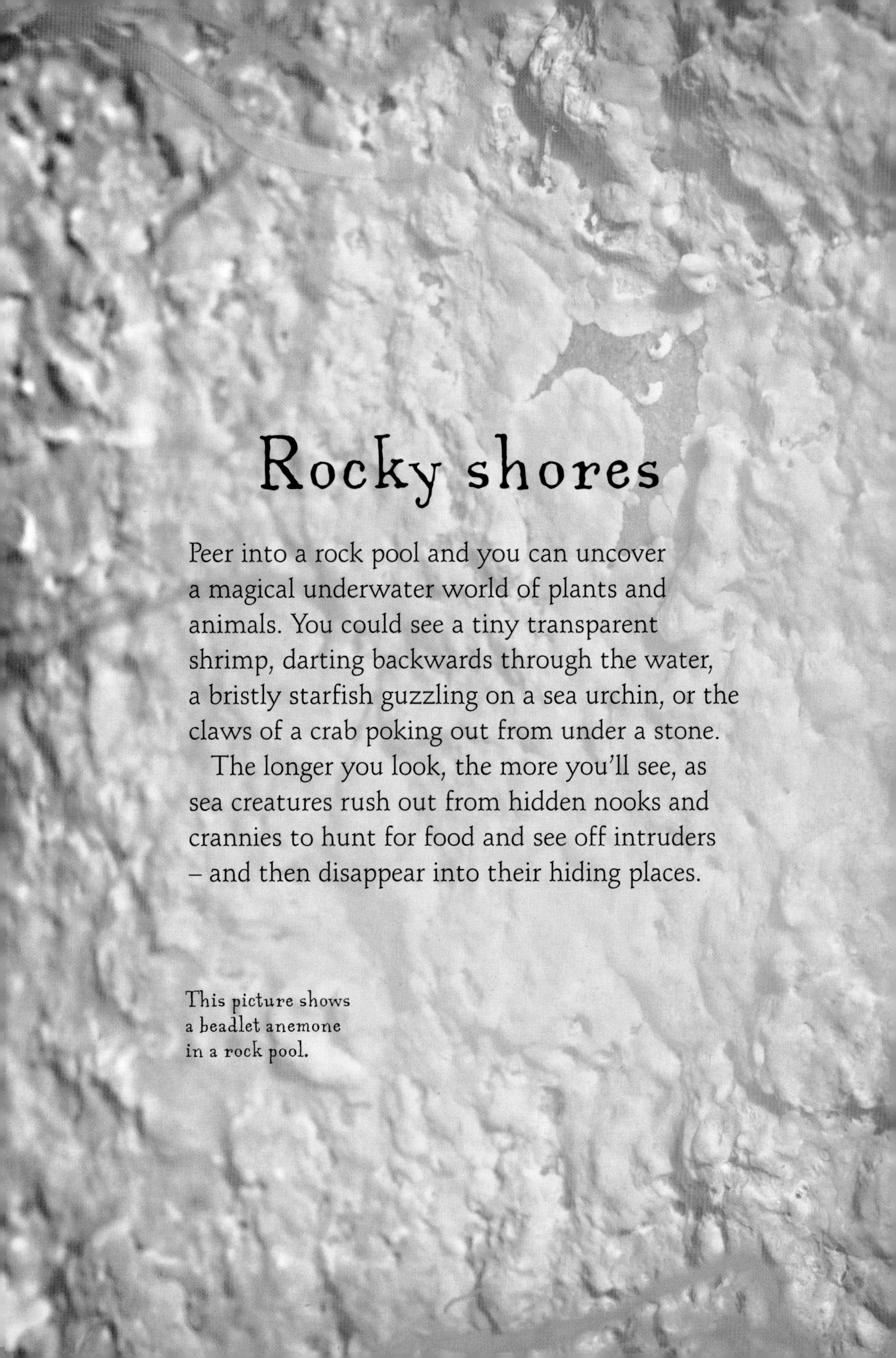

This picture shows
a beadlet anemone
in a rock pool.

TOP TIP

Over the course of the year, some creatures move higher or lower down the beach. So each time you look in a rock pool, you may see new animals there.

Inside a rock pool

Each rock pool is different. At the top of the beach, rock pools can be cut off from the sea for hours, or sometimes days, at a time. So living in one of these pools can be tough.

On a hot day, water from the pools evaporates, making the water left behind very salty. Sometimes it dries up altogether. When it rains, fresh water fills the pools, which is stressful for animals that are used to salt water. Creatures that live here have to be tough to survive these extreme conditions.

The nearer you get to the sea, the more often the tide fills the rock pools, making them much easier to live in.

Barnacles

Common mussels

Sea urchin

Small fish shelter from waves in rock pools.

A hermit crab lives inside a whelk shell.

Make a rock pool viewer

When you're looking into a rock pool, reflections on the surface can make it hard to see into the water. It's easy to make a simple viewer to help you see more clearly. For this you'll need an ice-cream carton, clingfilm and a pair of scissors.

1. Cut out the bottom of the carton.

2. Cut out the centre of the lid.

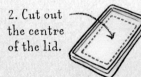

3. Stretch the clingfilm across the top of the tub and fix in place with the lid.

4. Simply press the viewer, clingfilm side down, to the surface of the water.

SNORKELLING

If you have a snorkelling mask, you could use it as an underwater viewer. Put on your mask and snorkel, and dip your head into the rock pool.

HANDY HINT

Take an old towel on your rock pool adventures. That way when you kneel down you won't cut yourself on sharp rocks or barnacles.

Sea anemones

Common white shrimp

Common shore crab

Butterfish

Periwinkle

Starfish

If you find a starfish inside a rock pool, you'll see straight away that it has no head or eyes. It also has no brain, but it will have at least five arms – and some have more than 30. On the underside of each one you can make out tiny tube feet, just like those of a sea urchin. They allow the starfish to crawl slowly across the ocean floor.

Super stomachs

All starfish eat other animals. If you find one wrapped around a creature with a shell, it's probably feeding. It uses its tube feet to pull the shell apart. Then it turns its own stomach inside out and pushes it into the shell, to suck up the soft body inside.

This common starfish is about to eat a mussel.

Starfish to spot

Cushion star
2cm/0.8"
Has short, plump arms,
and a distinctive shape.
Its colour varies from
orange to green or grey.
Found in rock pools.

Small brittle star
3cm/1.2"
Greyish blue in colour,
with spiny, slender arms.
Find it under stones,
in shallow water and
in rock pools.

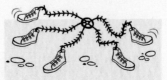

BRITTLE STARS
Brittle stars are
related to starfish.
They have round
bodies and long,
flexible arms, which
they use to 'walk'
across the ocean floor.

Common brittle star
Up to 8cm/3"
Very long arms and a
large circular body. Be
careful not to touch it
– it's very fragile,
and its arms can
easily break.

Sunstar
Up to 8cm/3"
Has many arms,
sometimes as many as 15.
Large, spiny and reddish
in colour. Eats other
starfish.

Common starfish
Up to 10cm/4"
Those living offshore can
grow up to 50cm long, but
smaller ones can be found
on beaches and in rock
pools. Five arms,
with bumpy spines.

Spiny starfish
Up to 12cm/4.7"
Easily identified by its
large spines. Usually
lives out to sea, but can
be found in rock pools
at low tide.

Black brittle star
Up to 15cm/6"
Black or brown,
sometimes found with
common brittle stars.
Feeds on algae or dead
meat.

Purple sunstar
Up to 8cm/3"
Has 7-13 arms, set
around a large disc.
Spiny surface.

A sea anemone on land. Its body is curled up to keep moisture inside.

A sea anemone in the water. Its tentacles are ready to catch prey.

Sea anemones

If you come across a sea anemone in a rock pool at low tide, squashed up into a slimy little ball, you probably won't be impressed. But at high tide, it's a different story.

Underwater, the anemone opens up like a strange and beautiful flower, revealing long, brightly coloured tentacles. But don't be fooled. It may look like a flower to us, but for many creatures it's a real-life sea monster. The anemone waits for the prey to swim close, then stings it with its tentacles. Next, it pulls the victim into its large stomach to be digested.

DANGEROUS TENTACLES

Be careful not to touch the tentacles of a sea anemone. They're covered in tiny cells that shoot poisoned harpoons into anything that touches them.

harpoon coiled inside the cell

harpoon shoots out

This jewel anemone is waiting to catch a passing fish.

A small fish swims within range of the sea anemone's deadly tentacles.

The fish is stung and pulled inside the anemone's mouth.

Sea anemones to spot

Beadlet anemone
3cm/1.2"

Can be identified by bright blue 'beads' just under the tentacles. Its body is usually red or green. Found in rock pools.

Wartlet anemone
4cm/1.6"

Six lines of white warts run up sides of its column, making it easy to identify at low tide. Underwater, look for its striped tentacles.

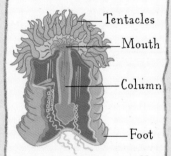
Hermit crab anemone
5cm/2"

This anemone lives on the shells of hermit crabs, and feeds on the crab's leftovers. It has a strong sucker to attach itself to the shell.

Daisy anemone
5cm/2"

Has lots of very short tentacles, just like a daisy's short petals. Common in rock crevices and in muddy areas.

Plumose anemone
7cm/2.8"

It has dense, very fine tentacles, making it appear fluffy. Usually orange or white in colour.

Snakelocks anemone
8cm/3"

Gets its name from its snakelike tentacles. Grey or green in colour, its tentacles are often tipped with purple.

Dahlia anemone
8cm/3"

Its body is covered in warts, making it difficult to see in rock pools. Its tentacles are arranged in short, squat bunches.

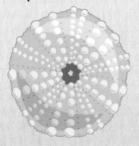
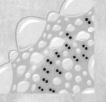
Sea urchins

The sea is home to many weird creatures, but few as strange as sea urchins. Look out for a sea urchin skeleton, called a test, lying on the beach. Here it looks innocent enough – a brittle, bumpy shell shaped like a ball. But a real live sea urchin is covered in long, poisonous spines that can give even humans a nasty injury.

Feeding

The sea urchin's spines are the ultimate protection, making it really unpleasant to eat. They can even move to point towards a predator. This leaves the sea urchin free to feast on its favourite food – algae. Its mouth is underneath its body, ringed by five sharp teeth.

A sea urchin feeding on algae

Sea urchins to spot

Sea urchins can be found in rockpools and in the shallows, although many live much further out to sea. If you find one, don't pick it up with your hands – you might get a painful sting. Instead, use a net to pop it into a tank. Then you'll be able to look at it close up. Between its spines, you'll notice hundreds of tiny tube-like feet, that it uses to move and stick to rocks. Here are some sea urchins to look out for.

Small purple-tipped sea urchin
Up to 4cm/1.6"
Common under rocks and stones close to the sea. Its green spines have purple tips. Sometimes known as a shore urchin.

Sea potato
5cm/2"
Lives in sand, leaving small, paw-shaped marks. Covered in short brown spines which make it appear hairy.

Black sea urchin
Up to 10cm/4"
Black spines with a greenish or reddish sheen. Lower zone and deep water. Not in Britain.

Edible sea urchin
Up to 15cm/6"
Easily identifiable by its size, and by its reddish coloured spines. Often eaten as a seafood delicacy.

PREDATORS

Despite its spines, the sea urchin has some predators.

*Lobsters break open sea urchins with their powerful claws.

*In the North Pacific, sea otters use rocks to crack open sea urchins and get to the soft flesh inside.

*In France, some people eat the sea urchin's bright orange eggs, cutting the urchin open to get at the eggs inside.

URCHIN ATTACK

Sea urchins usually stay in the same place, but sometimes hundreds of urchins all swarm together across the sea floor. They feed as they move, eating up seaweed on their way, leaving behind a bare sea bed.

Crabs and lobsters

They look like the scariest predators on the seashore, with huge pincers and tough armour plating. But crabs and lobsters are actually shy creatures that spend most of the day hiding. You might find a crab glistening in a rock pool, or even catch sight of one scuttling sideways across the sand.

Crab clues

If you don't see a live crab, you can still find clues that show where they've been. Look out for an empty shell, or 'carapace', left on the sand. About once a year, crabs shed their shells to grow bigger. Then they hide until a new one grows. Collecting carapaces is a good way to learn about different crab species.

Crab carapaces

CRAB HANDLING

Take care when picking up a crab – their pincers can give you a painful nip. Wear some gloves if it's your first try. Be careful not to damage your crab by squeezing too tightly.

1. Using your index finger, press down on top of the crab.

2. Place your thumb and middle finger on either side of its shell.

3. Lift the crab gently upwards.

This is a hermit crab. You can recognize it easily because it doesn't have its own shell. Instead, it lives in the old shell of another animal.

Going crabbing

The best way to get up close and personal with a crab is to go crabbing. You'll need a long piece of string, some bait (pieces of bacon will do), a small weight (a coin or something similar), and a clear plastic tank to put your catch in. You might also find a net helpful for scooping up crabs.

1. Tie the weight and bait onto one end of the string. A length of around 3m (10ft) is enough.

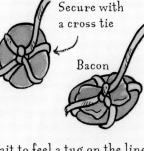

Secure with a cross tie

Bacon

2. Cast the weighted end of the string into the water.

3. Wait to feel a tug on the line, then slowly pull your crab in and put it in the tank, using your net if necessary.

4. When you've finished, release the crabs back into the sea.

When you go crabbing, you'll probably find all sorts of creatures racing to eat up your bait. Many rock pool creatures are scavengers, and will eat whatever they can find. The best kind of bait is the smelliest, as many seashore creatures have a very strong sense of smell.

Unlike lobsters, which hunt for their food, crabs are almost all scavengers. This means that they feed on plants and animals that have already died. Crabs will eat anything they can get their claws on, including:

Plankton (microscopic plants)

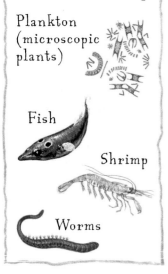

Fish

Shrimp

Worms

Common crabs and lobsters

Here are some crabs and lobsters that you might spot on the shore. The best time to look is at low tide, when many of them are left behind in small rock pools.

Check under seaweed and stones, as crabs will hide under anything to avoid predators, and even burrow into sand to stay out of danger. You'd have to be very lucky to spot a lobster, as they mostly live on the seabed.

Porcelain crab
1.2cm/0.5"
This tiny crab has a rounded body and its back legs are covered in hairs. It lives among stones close to the sea.

Hairy crab
2cm/0.8"
Its fine hairs trap dirt, helping it to blend into the background. When danger is close, it freezes and waits for the predator to leave.

Furrowed crab
2.5cm/1"
It has eight blunt 'teeth' on its furrowed shell. When approached, it extends its large claws so that it looks bigger.

Toothed pirimela
2.5cm/1"
The front of its shell has several 'teeth'. It has small pincers and lives in rocky areas in the lower zone.

Pennant's crab
3.5cm/1.4"
A strong swimmer. It uses its rear legs to propel itself in the water. It is found in shallows on sandy beaches.

Shore crab
4cm/1.6"
An aggressive species with a particularly broad shell. Very common. It lives in shallow water on rocky and sandy shores.

Squat lobster
4cm/1.6"
It has a short, flattened body, and very long claws for catching fish. It can be found on most British shorelines.

Sponge crab
7cm/2.8"
A rare crab. Its coat of hair makes it look furry. It gets its name from its habit of carrying pieces of sponge on its back.

Velvet swimming crab
8cm/3.2"
Attacks and eats other crabs. It has red eyes and its shell is covered with soft, velvety hair. Common around all British coasts.

Common hermit crab
10cm/3.9"
Lives all over the world. Hermit crabs often fight over the best shells to live in. When they outgrow their shells, they move into another one.

Edible crab
11cm/4.3"
Bright orange crab with a very broad oval shell. Look out for its distinctive long, black-tipped claws.

Thornback spider crab
15cm/6"
The spiny shell of the thornback spider crab makes it easy to recognize. It also has particularly long legs.

Common lobster
45cm/17.7"
Can sometimes be found in rock pools on British shores. It uses its pincers for crushing and cutting up prey.

*FANTASTIC FACT *
Many people think that lobsters are red, but really most are a blue-black colour. This makes them hard to see on the ocean floor. Lobsters only turn red when they are boiled to be eaten as seafood.

Crustaceans

Barnacles, shrimps and prawns all come
from the same group of animals as crabs
and lobsters: crustaceans. They might look
very different, but they all have hard shells,
jointed bodies and a pair of antennae.

Shrimps and prawns can be tricky to spot,
as they can move very fast. Barnacles are
much easier to find – they don't move at all.
Here are some crustaceans to look out for.

Star barnacle
1.2cm/0.5"
Slightly smaller than an
acorn barnacle. When
underwater, the shell
opens up and its tiny legs
stretch out to feed.

Acorn barnacle
1.5cm/0.5"
Has a diamond-shaped
opening in its shell.
When underwater,
legs protrude from its
opening, catching food
that drifts past.

Sea slater
2.5cm/1"
Looks like a large
woodlouse. Moves down
the shore to feed on dead
matter around rocks as
the tide goes out.
Runs fast.

Chameleon prawn
Up to 3cm/1"
Lives among seaweed in
lower zone rock pools
or in shallow water.
Changes colour to blend
into its surroundings.

Common shrimp
Up to 5cm/2"
Very well camouflaged.
Has broad, flattened
claws on its first legs.
Also found on sandy
shores, where it buries
itself in the sand.

Common prawn
Up to 10cm/4"
Nearly transparent body,
with long feelers. Some
have bright blue and
yellow markings on
their legs. Feeds on dead
matter in rock pools.

Sponges and corals

Some sponges look like footballs, some look like chimneys, and some look like brains – but sponges are actually very simple animals.

Look out for them in rock pools and on the lower shore. You might see corals too. Corals also look like weird and wonderful plants, but they are actually colonies of lots of tiny animals. Here are some sponges and corals to spot.

SPIKY SPONGES

Since sponges move very little, they have developed good ways to defend themselves. Some have spikes to make them hard to eat, others produce toxic chemicals to repel predators.

Cup coral
3cm/1"
Can be white, pink, orange, red or green. One animal is found in each cup-shaped skeleton. On rocks on the lower zone.

Scyphia ciliata
Up to 5cm/2" tall
Hairy, upright tube, often with fringed top. Found under overhangs or attached to rocks and shells. Also grows on seaweeds.

Sea orange
Up to 7cm/3"
Large, round, orange, yellow or white sponge, also known as a 'brain sponge'. In shallow water or offshore.

Bread sponge
10cm across/4"
Green or yellow sponge. Many different shapes. Crumbles when handled. Found on lower zone on rocks and shells.

Mermaid's glove
Up to 16cm/6"
Looks like a small tree. Can be yellowish, green, pink or purple. Often found in silty areas.

Sea fan
Up to 50cm/20"
Pale pink coral. Individuals can be seen on branches. Found on rocks in shallow water or washed ashore.

A sandy beach may look all the same on the surface, but it has zones, just like a rocky shore. You'll find different creatures on different parts of the beach.

Sandy shores

You might walk along a sandy beach without
seeing a single living thing. But lots of seashore
creatures live on sandy shores – it's just that
they're out of sight. Many of the smaller animals
that live here could get gobbled up by a bird or
a fish. So they bury themselves into the sand to
stay out of danger.

   If you start digging, you could find all sorts of
animals, from long, wriggly worms to curious
looking shells and even prickly sea urchins buried
below the surface.

You can bring razor shells to the surface with this simple trick. All you need is a few pinches of salt.

1. Sprinkle a pinch of salt down the razor shell's burrow.

2. If there's a razor shell there, it will think the tide has come in, and come to the surface.

3. As it surfaces, take hold of it and pull it out of its burrow.

4. When you've looked at it, put the razor shell back on the sand, and watch the curious way it burrows back down.

1 2 3 4

Secrets in the sand

Look closely at the surface of a sandy beach and you will find clues that lead you to the creatures living in the sand. Some seashore animals are excellent diggers, disappearing into the sand at top speed when they're in danger. And when the tide is out, they stay under the surface where the sand is wetter.

Dig gently and sift through the sand and mud to find the animals before they burrow away.

A sand mason is a worm that lives inside a tube made of sand.

A lugworm cast shows the entrance to its burrow.

Snipe

Lugworm

Trough shells

A purple heart urchin buries itself deep into the sand.

Burrowing tube

You might think it would be hard to find any animal as boring as a worm. But seashore worms can be much more exotic looking than the simple earthworm. The sand mason, for example, builds a tube out of sand and tiny pieces of shell around itself. Here are some more worms to look out for:

Lugworms are fat and brown. Look closely to see the tiny gills along their bodies.

Ragworms have red lines down their backs and blue bristles along their sides.

Ribbon worms can be brown or purple and grow up to 30 metres (100ft) long.

Netted whelk

Sand gapers bury themselves deeper as they grow larger.

Masked crabs stay near the surface.

A razor shell in its burrow

BURROWING TUBE

If you want to see how worms burrow, you could make a viewing tube. All you need is:

*Empty plastic drinks bottle
*Gaffer tape
*Scissors

1. Cut off the top and bottom of the bottle.

You need this bit

2. Flatten the bottle.

3. Tape up the bottom with gaffer tape.

4. Once you've found a worm, fill the viewer with sand from the spot where you found it.

5. Now place the worm on the surface of the sand and watch as it burrows.

WEATHER FORECAST

Sea belt is a type of seaweed that can help you to predict the weather. If it's limp and wet, rain is coming. If it's dry and crisp, warm weather is on the way.

Sea belt looks like a ribbon with wavy edges.

Seaweed

There's one living thing you're certain to see on the shore, but it's not an animal, and it's not a plant, either. It's seaweed – part of a group of living things called algae. Most algae look like plants, and even behave like plants, but they have no roots, flowers or leaves.

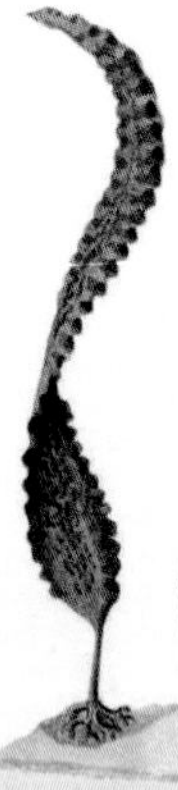

Seaweed gets its energy from the Sun, so you'll find it close to the surface of the water, where there's plenty of sunlight. For some creatures it's a good place to hide, and for others it's a tasty dinner. There are three different colours to spot: green, brown and red.

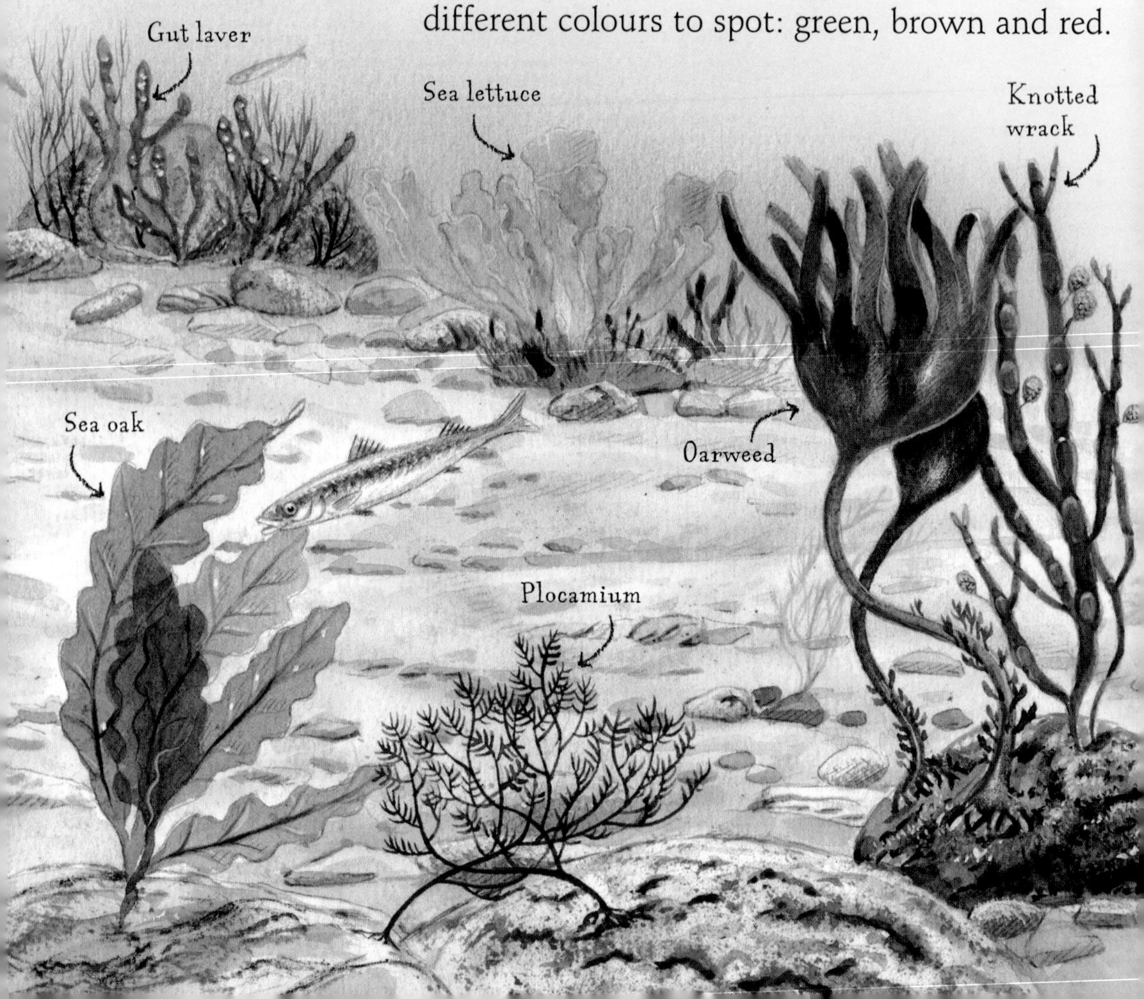

Gut laver
Sea lettuce
Knotted wrack
Sea oak
Oarweed
Plocamium

This is a brown seaweed called bladder wrack.

The vein in the middle of a frond is called a midrib.

Air pockets, or bladders, help to keep it afloat – just like a lifejacket.

Disc-shaped holdfast

Look closely at each frond – you might spot another plant growing on it.

Tiny animals such as molluscs or worms live on fronds.

STAYING PUT

Seaweeds are specially adapted to stand up to rough waves. Most have a 'holdfast', which helps them to grip onto rocks.

These disc-shaped and button-shaped holdfasts glue onto the rock face.

Branched holdfasts have tentacle-like strands that creep into small spaces and hold on tight.

DID YOU KNOW?

Microscopic algae sometimes 'bloom', growing so fast that they make the sea change colour. This is called a 'red tide', and can turn the water blood red.

Giant algae

There are all kinds of algae living in the sea. Most are tiny – like the microscopic plankton that is a favourite food for many fish. Some, however, are gigantic. The monstrous giant kelp is a seaweed that can be 100m (330ft) long and grows at up to 60cm (2ft) every day.

TOP TIPS

* Here's a simple trick to help you identify seaweed: hold it underwater. The shape of the fronds will be much clearer.

* Keep a look out for mussels clinging to seaweed. This shows that the seaweed has been around for a while – a year, at least.

* Watch out for hornwrack. It looks like seaweed, but is really the remains of a colony of very small creatures.

Seaweed to spot

The best time to hunt for seaweed is just after a storm. You'll find plenty washed up on the beach, and many that normally live too far out to see. Some will have broken off from their holdfasts, so you'll need to look at the fronds to identify them. If you find a whole one, try giving it a tug, to see how well the holdfast keeps it in place. Take care not to pull it off.

Maerl
7cm/2.8"
This red seaweed has a tough coating of lime. It can be smooth or flaky, and grows like a crust on rocks and stones.

Bryopsis
7.5cm/3"
Bryopsis looks shiny and feathery. It grows in clumps on the sides of rock pools in the middle and lower zones.

Channelled wrack
10cm/4"
This brown seaweed can survive for days out of the water. The edges of its fronds curve in to form channels that keep water inside.

Purple laver
15cm/6"
Purple lavers have wide, smooth fronds, attached to a small, disc-shaped holdfast. They live on sand-covered stones, in the middle and lower shores.

Irish moss
15cm/6"

Irish moss has a disc-shaped holdfast, and varies from green to purple in colour.

Plocamium
15-20cm/6-8"

A distinctive red seaweed, it has feathery tips growing on one side of each fine frond.

Sea oak
20cm/8"

Fronds look like bright red oak leaves. Sea oaks often grow on the stalks of large brown seaweeds.

Gut weed
20cm/8"

Gut weed is common on all British coasts. It has tube-like fronds which are inflated like balloons. Lives in the upper zone.

Sea lettuce
20cm/8"

This green seaweed is extremely common on rocky shores in Britain. As it ages, its fronds become darker in colour.

Bladder wrack
60cm/24"

This tough, strap-like seaweed grips on to rocks with a root-like holdfast. It has pairs of air bladders to keep it afloat.

Knotted wrack
1m/39"

It has a round stem, but the fronds become flat further up. It has small air bladders, and can be found on rocks on the middle zone.

Oarweed
1.5m/59"

This hardy brown seaweed has a wide blade with flat strips called 'digits', that look like oars.

FANTASTIC FACT

Many seaweeds can be eaten, if they've been prepared carefully. In Japan, seaweed is made into papery sheets called nori. These can be flavoured and eaten as a snack, or used to wrap up raw fish.

Flowers and grasses

Most people think of the seaside as a relaxing place for a holiday, but for the plants that live there, it's a battle to survive. Each part of the seashore has different challenges.

Clifftop plants are buffeted by fierce winds. Plants on shingle beaches struggle to stay rooted, as the soil is constantly shifted by the tide. Those near the sea are showered with salt water, which damages most plants.

Look carefully, and you can sometimes spot how these hardy survivors have adapted to the harsh conditions.

The yellow horned poppy has thick leaves that are covered in fine hairs, to trap rainwater.

Shrubby sea blite

The fleshy leaves of the golden samphire help it conserve water.

Sea pea

Sea kale has winding, extra-long roots to help it stay in place on shifting shingle beaches.

On clifftops, winds can be so strong that they force trees to grow into strange, twisted shapes.

Marram grass is easy to find on a sandy beach. In fact, its scientific name is ammophilia, which means 'sand lover'. It has adapted in very clever ways to its harsh habitat.

In dry weather, most plants lose a lot of water into the air. But marram grass can curl up its leaves, which stops the water from escaping.

Its long, flexible stems bend with the wind, instead of snapping.

Sand dunes

Marram grass is one of the best survivors of all. It's one of the very few plants that can live on sandy beaches. Here water is scarce, winds are strong and the ground is unsteady. However, once marram grass has taken root, sand dunes will begin to form, allowing more delicate plants to grow there too.

Sea sandwort can be found in sand dunes. It helps to stop the sand drifting.

Sea lavender can survive in muddy saltmarshes as well as sand dunes.

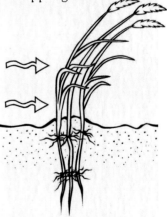

It also has long roots, which can reach down for water below the sand.

49

Flowers and grasses to spot

There aren't as many plants to spot on the shore as there are inland – so it's a lot easier to tell one from another. Look at the shape of the leaves, and the colour and shape of the whole plant.

It's best to go spotting in the summer, when you'll see clouds of pink and purple flowers, gently swaying in the breeze.

MAGIC FLOWERS

Dune gentians are named after Gentius, a pirate king. According to legend, Gentius was the first person to discover that these plants could help cure illnesses. Gentians are used in medicines for everything from helping digestion to curing certain snake bites.

Bird's foot trefoil
10cm/4"
Sometimes called 'bacon and eggs' because of the yellow and red in its flowers. Grows in clumps on grassy banks or cliffs.

Buckshorn plantain
10cm/4"
This hardy plant has hairy leaves that grow close to the ground. Look for it on gravelly areas close to the sea.

Thrift
15cm/6"
Thrift, or 'sea pink', grows in low-lying clumps. It can be seen on rocky cliffs and flowers from March to September.

Sea arrowgrass
15-50cm/6-20"
It has flat, spiky leaves and is found on grassy salt marshes. Small green flowers appear from May to August.

Sea campion
20cm/8"
Grows in big cushion-like tufts. Common on cliffs and shingle beaches, and flowers June to August.

Annual seablite
20cm/8"
Very thick, fleshy leaves.
Grows along the ground
or upright. Look out
for it on muddy
and sandy shores.

Sea milkwort
Up to 25cm/10"
The pretty pink flowers
of this creeping
plant can be
seen on grassy
salt marshes.
Flowers June
to August.

Sea sandwort
30cm/12"
Found on sand and
shingle beaches. Small
white flowers. Very
common. Flowers May
to August.

Sea lavender
Up to 40cm/16"
Lots of purple flowers,
with the leaves in a group
close to the ground.
This tough
plant grows
in salt marshes
and flowers
July to
September.

Sea holly
Up to 50cm/20"
Prickly green leaves
which turn white in the
winter. Its tiny blue
flowers attract butterflies.
Found on sand
and shingle.

Sea wormwood
50cm/20"
Sea wormwood, or
'old woman', grows
in estuaries above
the tide level. It has
grey-green leaves
that are covered
in a soft
down.

Sea kale
Up to 1m/39"
Large, cabbage-like
leaves with crinkly edges.
Sea kale grows on shingle
beaches and flowers June
to August.

Yellow horned poppy
Up to 1m/39"
Brightly coloured.
Has a long, green seed
pod which looks like a
horn. Flowers June to
September.

Marram grass
Up to 1.2m/47"
One of the hardiest
plants on the
seashore. Common
on sand dunes
on most
British shores.

Sand dunes

All kinds of wildlife lives in sand dunes, from rabbits nibbling at grass to bright green dragonflies whirring through the air, and skylarks singing high in the sky.

The best time of year to visit is the summer, when you might see bright blue butterflies, lizards or adders basking in the sun.

Looking for clues

You might walk through a sand dune and see no wildlife at all, but you'll still be able to list several birds and animals that live there, from the clues they've left behind.

Dragonfly

Listen out for skylarks. They make a high warbling song.

Cinnabar moth

Animal hair stuck to a fence

Pellets outside this rabbit burrow show that it is still being used.

Moth larvae

A sand lizard basks in the sun.

The night watch

The best time to spot mammals on a sand dune is after dark. If you can persuade an adult to take you night watching, you might hear a hedgehog shuffling past, or even come face to face with a fox.

1. In the daytime, look for clues to find out what animals are living in the dune.

2. Find a couple of good viewpoints. Ideally, you should be as hidden as possible.

3. When you return at night, check the wind direction by throwing dust in the air and seeing which way it falls.

Wind direction

4. Go to a viewpoint downwind of the spot you want to watch.

5. Now you can begin. Keep as still as possible, and record your sightings in a notebook.

June 30th
Waited for about half an hour. Then a fox came out of its set, followed by two little cubs. The cubs played around, but both soon disappeared back down the hole. The adult fox started nosing around, began eating something, and then bolted. After it had gone, I saw it had been eating a bird's egg.

DANGER DANGER

When animals sense danger, they freeze, then run for cover. Follow these tips so that you can watch animals without them being aware of you.

Always be as quiet as you can when observing animals.

Approach an animal by moving as slowly as possible.

Try and remain downwind of the animal, so your scent doesn't reach it.

STUFF TO TAKE

Torch, covered with a piece of red plastic (red light frightens animals less than white light)

Notebook and pencil

Dark clothing

Cushion to sit on

Food and drink

Sand dune creatures to spot

What you'll spot in a sand dune depends on what time of day you go. In the daytime, look out for adders and lizards. They both bask in the sun until their bodies are warm enough to hunt for food. Stoats and rabbits appear just after dusk, and you're more likely to see foxes or hedgehogs at night.

Here are some creatures to look out for.

Wolf spider
0.5cm/0.1-0.2"
Builds a silk-lined burrow in the ground or in a disused rabbit hole, and waits inside to pounce on its prey.

Sand wasp
2cm/0.5"
Makes its nest in the sand. Paralyses a caterpillar and lays its egg on top of it, and then seals the nest with sand. Flies May to August.

Common blue butterfly
Wingspan 3cm/1.5"
Size and markings vary. Caterpillar eats bird's foot trefoil.

Blue tailed damselfly
Wingspan 3.5cm/1.5"
Body is all black with a blue segment near the end. Found on plants in sand dunes. Common. Seen from May to September.

Meadow brown butterfly
Wingspan 5cm/2"
Eats brambles, knapweed and thistles. Caterpillar eats grasses.

Golden-ringed dragonfly
Wingspan 9cm/3.5"
Large dragonfly with green eyes and black body marked with gold rings.

Emperor dragonfly
Wingspan 10cm/4"
Male is bright turquoise, female is dull green. Dark line runs down the centre of the body.

Common lizard
Up to 18cm/7"
Brown, green or bronze back with darker sides. Male has orange belly. Female has cream belly. Hibernates from October to March.

Stoat
16-31cm/6-12"
Brown in summer, with a lighter underside. Coat turns white in winter. Lives in burrows.

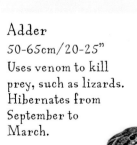

Skylark
30cm/12"
Small, streaky brown bird, with a small crest that it raises when alarmed. Makes a melodious warbling song.

Kestrel
34cm/13"
Has a long tail, pointed wings, and hovers above dunes while hunting. Makes a piercing "kee-kee-kee" call.

Adder
50-65cm/20-25"
Uses venom to kill prey, such as lizards. Hibernates from September to March.

Common buzzard
54cm/21"
Large bird of prey, with broad, rounded wings. It flies above dunes, searching for rabbits and other small mammals to catch.

Cockle shells like these
can be found on sandy
and muddy shores.

Shells

Molluscs are small, soft-bodied creatures, which include snails and oysters. The seashore is a tough place to survive, with animals and birds on the lookout for a juicy meal, and pounding waves to sweep them away.

That's why molluscs live in their own personal fortresses – shells. Molluscs that move along the sand have 'grips' on their shells, that help them move faster. Others, such as razor shells, have smooth shells that allow them to burrow quickly into the sand. Some shells even have sharp 'teeth' at their entrances to keep predators at bay.

Single shelled
molluscs are called
uni-valves.

Molluscs called
bi-valves have two
shells that are joined
together with a hinge.

Some molluscs, such
as squid, have shells
inside their bodies.

A squid's shell
is called a pen.

Chitons are molluscs
with eight plates
over an oval body.

Shore wars

Shells help to keep molluscs safe from
predators. But seashore creatures still try
to gobble them up, so molluscs need a few
extra tricks to get away. Dog whelks are
small molluscs that look like tasty snacks
to starfish. When starfish attack them, the
whelks rock violently from side to side to
shake off their attackers.

Some molluscs even eat other molluscs. Dog
whelks eat smaller molluscs called mussels.
They drill through the mussel's shell and suck
out the soft insides. But mussels have a great
trick to defend themselves. While the dog
whelk is drilling away, the mussel produces
sticky threads and ties the dog whelk to
the rock. The dog whelk gets stuck and the
mussel escapes.

This mollusc is called a scallop.
It releases sticky threads
to attach itself to
the seabed.

Limpet trail

Limpets are small molluscs often found on rocks. If you look at a few limpets, stuck to the side of a rock pool, you might think that they don't move at all. But you'd be wrong.

You can find out what they get up to with a simple experiment – without having to stare at a rock for hours on end. For this you need a paintbrush, some different coloured oil-based paints, a notebook and coloured pencils. Just follow these simple steps:

1. At low tide, mark several limpets with different coloured blobs of paint.

2. Make a map of their positions.

3. Return after the next high tide, and see what has happened. Have they moved at all? Do some swap places?

4. You could try moving a limpet yourself to a nearby rock. Come back the next day, and find out if it has made its way home.

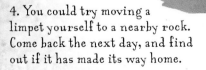

yesterday

today

5. See if you can spot any markings on the rock. Limpets grind the rock down so they fit snugly to it, making a dent called a 'home scar'.

PICK UP A LIMPET

When limpets feel vibrations, they clamp themselves tightly down onto the rock. But if you walk up to a limpet as quietly as possible, you can catch one with its shell slightly raised. Then pick it up and pop it in a tank or jar to see the animal inside.

SEA WATER SUPPER

Bi-valve molluscs feed on the nutrients in sea water. They have two siphons, and they suck in water through one and shoot out waste through the other. Put some bi-valve molluscs in a transparent tank, look closely and you'll see them in action.

HANDY HINT

1. When you've taken them home, wash your shells with a toothbrush and warm water. Coat them with baby oil, to stop the colours from fading.

2. Identify your shells, then label each one with its name, date and where you found it.

3. Store your shells away from strong sunlight.

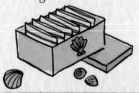

Collecting shells

Collecting shells can be a great way to get to know the different species. When you find a shell, check that there isn't a mollusc still living inside it. If you're not sure, put the shell in a jar or tank full of water, and wait to see if anything peeps out of the shell entrance. If there is a live mollusc inside it, put the shell back where you found it.

If the shell is empty, first write down where you found it. Was it in the sand, under some seaweed, or in a rock pool? Do you know what zone it was in? What other plants and animals are nearby? All this can help you to identify it.

These screw shells live in shallow water, and are sometimes washed up onto the beach.

Shells to spot

Flat periwinkle
1cm/0.4"
Small and rounded winkle. Colour can vary from white to yellow, orange, brown and black. Feeds on seaweed.

Common periwinkle
2.5cm/1"
Shell is shaped like a snail. Can be brown or black. Feeds on seaweed. Found on rocky shores and estuaries.

Dog whelk
3cm/1"
Pale, grey or white spiral shell. It breaks open barnacles or bores through mussel shells to feed on them.

Netted dog whelk
up to 3cm/1.5"
Very common on rocky and sandy shores. Conical shell, with spiral ridges. Feeds on carrion, such as dead fish or crabs.

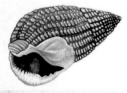

Saddle oyster
6cm/2.5"
Two valves have different shapes. One resembles a saddle. Found on rocks on the middle and lower zone.

Common limpet
up to 6cm/2.5"
Can be found on almost any seashore. Clings to rocks, and crawls around at high tide, feeding off algae.

Common mussel
1-10cm/0.5-4"
These live in large groups on rocky shores, anchoring themselves to rocks and to each other with sticky threads.

Common oyster
10cm/4"
The two halves of the shell are different shapes. The inside is pale blue or white; the outside is scaly. Found in shallow water.

Common whelk
Up to 11cm/4.5"
Huge whelk, found on sandy, muddy and rocky shores. Flat oval on its foot acts as a 'door' across the shell's entrance.

Looking at shells

Shells have beautiful patterns and intricate shapes, but they're not just for show. Each shell is adapted for the mollusc that lives in it.

When you find a shell, look at its shape. Is it smooth, to help the shell slip into the sand? Is it ridged, to help the shell get a grip on the seabed? Can you see any holes in it? These could have been caused by a predator. Here are some shells to look out for.

Chink shell
Up to 1cm/0.5"
Pale with striped bands. Found on seaweed in lower zone and shallow water.

Purple topshell
Up to 2cm/1"
Empty shells washed up on shore. Red stripes. Common on all types of shore.

Tellin
Up to 2cm/1"
Pink or white, glossy shells. Burrows quickly into sand when the tide falls. Muddy and sandy shores and estuaries.

Banded wedge shell
Up to 3cm/1"
Thin, broad shell. Can be yellow, orange, pink or brown. Burrows in the sand. Sandy beaches.

Painted topshell
Up to 3cm/1"
Shell is often a yellowish, pinkish colour, with red stripes. Keeps its shell clean by rubbing it with its long foot.

Necklace shell
Up to 3cm/1"
Pale yellow. Eats other
molluscs by boring holes
in their shells and eating
the flesh inside. Usually
buried in the sand.

Common cockle
Up to 5cm/2"
Very common shell with
two valves. Ribs and
growth lines on shell.
Off-white, yellow
or brown.

Rayed trough shell
Up to 5cm/2"
Shell has pale rays
stretching across it.
Light purple inside.
Sandy or gravel
shores.

Pelican's foot
5.5cm/2"
Distinctive foot makes
it easy to spot. Found
on muddy and
sandy shores.

Screw shell
6cm/2.5"
Long, thin shell often
found on sandy bottoms
in deep water. Sometimes
washed ashore.

Common sand gaper
Up to 15cm/6"
Soft, thin shell, usually
stained black by a layer
in the mud. Sandy and
muddy shores.

White piddock
Up to 15cm/6"
Burrows into rock,
firm sand and wood,
using strong teeth at
the edge of its shell.

Razor shell
Up to 15cm/6"
Uses its muscular
foot to burrow
quickly into the
sand or mud when
the tide goes out.
Shell is smooth on
the outside, with
brown or reddish
markings.

Horse mussel
Up to 20cm/8"
Found on oarweed on
the lower shore, or in
the water. One of the
largest mussels
in Europe.

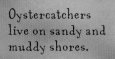
Oystercatchers
live on sandy and
muddy shores.

Birds

Look out to sea, and the chances are, you'll probably see a bird. While lots of seashore creatures are buried in the sand or hidden under rocks, seashore birds are easy to spot. To begin birdwatching, all you need to do is get into the habit of looking.

   Once you've started watching out for them, you'll begin to notice birds everywhere. There are lots of different species to spot, from oystercatchers, little black and white birds that fly low over the waves, to gannets, large white seabirds that divebomb into the ocean to catch fish.

Looking at birds

Even if you think you know nothing about birds, there will be some that you already recognize, such as gulls. You might think that gulls are pretty ordinary, humdrum birds. But they are hardy and intelligent, and there are lots of different kinds.

Sociable, noisy herring gulls are the easiest to spot. They thrive in seaside towns, plundering bins for food, and have even been seen walking into shops to steal packets of crisps. Kittiwakes are small, delicate looking gulls that spend the winter on the oceans without ever touching land, while black-backed gulls are hardy scavengers that eat anything they can find.

A lesser
black-backed gull

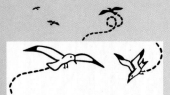

WING SHAPES

The shape of a bird's wing is adapted to how it flies.

Little terns have scythe-shaped wings for rapid flight.

Herring gulls have long, broad wings for gliding.

Kittiwakes use their curved wings for gliding too.

The right time

Some seashore birds migrate – they travel hundreds or thousands of miles each year to find the ideal spot to feed or raise their young. Arctic terns, for example, fly all the way from Europe to the Antarctic each year. So you'll only see some seabirds at certain times of year. Check in your field guide for the best times to spot each species.

Arctic terns can fly up to 22,000 miles each year.

The right place

As you get to know each habitat, you'll get to know where to find each species. On a muddy beach you could spot dozens of black and white birds called oystercatchers. But you won't see any on a rocky cliff. Oystercatchers find their food in thick, gloopy mud – on a cliff there's nothing for them to eat.

BRAINY BIRDS
When birds migrate, they navigate in lots of different ways. Some navigate by the Sun and stars and some use magnetic fields. But many birds also memorise their entire route. Arctic terns can fly 10,000 miles around the globe, and return to the same nesting site a year later.

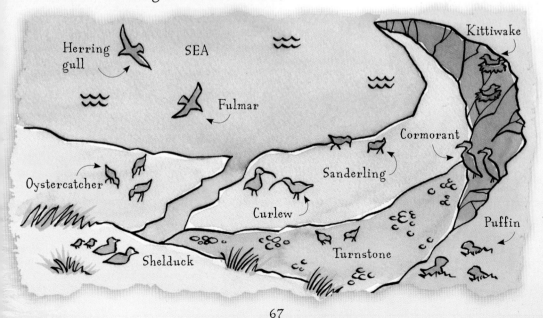

Herring gull

SEA

Kittiwake

Fulmar

Cormorant

Sanderling

Oystercatcher

Curlew

Puffin

Shelduck

Turnstone

67

Some birds change their feathers with the seasons.

Dunlin in winter

Summer

In some species, the males look different to the females.

Female

Shelduck male

KEY QUESTIONS

1. Look at its size, and compare it to a bird you know.

2. What shape is its beak? What colour is the bird?

3. What is it doing? Does it walk or hop? How does it fly?

4. What noise does it make?

5. Look up the bird in your field guide and see if you can identify it from your notes.

Identifying birds

At first, birds can be tricky to identify. On a muddy beach, you may see lots of birds, picking their way across the mud – and they often look confusingly similar. But if you look more closely, there are lots of ways to tell them apart. If you want to identify a bird, just keep looking at it, ask a few simple questions, and note down your answers.

Mystery bird

?

Blackbird

It's larger than a blackbird

Brown upperparts

Pale belly

Long legs

Its long bill curves downwards

It walked slowly, dipping its bill in the water.

It's a... CURLEW

Bird sounds

You can also learn to identify birds with your ears. Many seashore birds have distinctive calls. Lapwings, for example, cry "pee-wit, pee-wit", gannets cackle noisily and ringed plovers have a high, piping call. Birds have different calls to greet each other and alert other birds to danger. And, when they're trying to impress a potential mate, they burst into a noisy display.

To learn bird calls, look for a bird you know by sight, and write down what its call sounds like. Then you'll be able to identify it later, even if you can't see it.

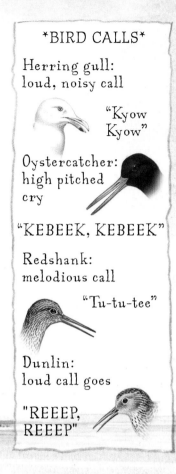

BIRD CALLS

Herring gull:
loud, noisy call

"Kyow
Kyow"

Oystercatcher:
high pitched
cry

"KEBEEK, KEBEEK"

Redshank:
melodious call

"Tu-tu-tee"

Dunlin:
loud call goes

"REEEP,
REEEP"

Snipe

Dunlin

Greenshank

Oystercatcher

Lapwing

TOP TIP

You could use a CD of bird calls to get to know them. You can also find websites with bird calls on the Usborne Quicklinks Website at www.usborne-quicklinks.com

Sandy beaches

Here are some of the birds you might see on a sandy beach. There are lots of wading birds and gulls to spot. The largest of these is the greater black-backed gull. It's a formidable predator that steals food from other birds, and sometimes swoops over cliffs and carries off another bird, such as a puffin, to eat.

Sanderling
20cm/8"
Small, energetic wading bird. Straight black bill and black legs. Pale grey wings and white underneath.

Lesser black-backed gull
53cm/21"
Adult has dark grey back and wings, bright yellow beak and yellow legs. All year round.

Herring gull
53cm/21"
Large, noisy gull, with pale grey back and wings and black and white wingtips. All year round.

Greater black-backed gull
66cm/26"
Very large, thick-set gull, with a slow, heavy flight. Kills and eats smaller birds. Large white spots on black tail. All year round.

Shingle beaches

Shingle beaches are covered in pebbles and make fantastic nesting sites for a lot of different birds. Some seabirds' eggs are speckled brown and grey, so they're well hidden among rocks and stones. In summer, look out for Arctic terns, beautiful birds that spend the summer in Europe before setting off for their winter home – the Antarctic.

FANTASTIC FACT
Ringed plovers use a cunning trick to protect their nests. If they spot a predator coming too close, they pretend to be injured, so that they seem easy to catch. They drag a wing along the ground and lure the predator away from their eggs or chicks.

Ringed plover
19cm/7.5"
Brown and grey upperparts, orange bill with a black tip. Black collar on white front. Runs in stops and starts. All year round.

Turnstone
23cm/9"
Brown and black upperparts, white underparts and orange legs. Can be seen turning over stones to find food underneath.

Arctic tern
34cm/13"
Silvery grey bird with a long tail, a black head and a blood red bill. Known as a 'sea swallow'. Graceful flight, often seen in flocks. Summer.

Common tern
34cm/13"
White with a black cap. Longer black-tipped bill, longer legs and a shorter tail than the similar Arctic tern. Summer.

Black-headed gull
37cm/14.5"
White head, with a dark smudge behind the eye in winter, dark brown head in summer. Nests in colonies. Also found inland.

Winter

WADERS' BILLS

Many wading birds' bills are adapted to help them find food in the mud.

Curlews' bills are very sensitive. They feel every vibration in the mud as they search for shellfish.

Snipe can open the tips of their bills when they are deep in the mud.

Dunlins use their short bills to pick up tiny snails and worms from the surface of the mud.

Muddy shores

Imagine a table laden with all the most delicious foods you can think of. That's what a muddy shore is like for a wader. Many waders feed on beaches and estuaries – the muddy channels where rivers flow into the sea. The mud is packed with shellfish, crabs and worms, so the birds flock there as the tide goes out, and frantically feed by dipping their beaks (also known as bills) in the mud.

At high tide you might see birds huddled at the top of the beach, waiting for the tide to drop so they can start feeding.

Lapwings run across the mud and pounce on anything that moves.

Shelducks find molluscs in the mud at low tide.

These dunlins are waiting for the tide to go out, so they can start eating.

Birds to spot

Dunlin
19cm/7"
Common, small wading bird with a down-curving beak, and a black belly patch in summer. Mostly autumn and winter.

Knot
25cm/10"
Grey in winter, with a pale eye stripe. In summer its chest, belly and face are red. Flies in huge flocks in winter. Autumn and winter.

Redshank
28cm/11"
Grey-brown with a long, straight bill and long red legs. White rear edges to wings are shown in flight. All year round.

Greenshank
30cm/12"
Similar size to a redshank, with a dark grey back, white underparts and pale green legs. Distinctive loud call. Spring and autumn.

Bar-tailed godwit
37cm/14"
Long-legged bird with grey-brown upperparts and paler belly. Has a long, up-turned red bill with a black tip. Most common in winter.

Avocet
43cm/17"
Rare, black and white bird with a long, up-curving bill. Feeds by sweeping bill from side to side in the water. All year round.

Oystercatcher
43cm/17"
Black and white with a bright orange bill and reddish legs. Jabs its bill into the mud to find food. Shows a white rump and wing stripe in flight. All year round.

Curlew
55cm/19-25"
Very large wading bird, with a down-curving beak, brown upperparts and long legs. White rump is noticeable in flight. All year round.

Shelduck
61cm/24"
White, orange and black duck with a dark green head and a bright red bill. Slow beating wings in flight. All year round.

PIRATE ALERT

Most seabirds catch fish for themselves, but great skuas chase other birds, force them to drop their catch, and then grab it for themselves.

FANTASTIC FACT

Gannets are well designed to hit the waves at speed. Their skulls act like crash helmets and they have a pocket in their throats that protects them like a car's airbag when they hit the water.

Cliff birds

Sea cliffs are fantastic places to spot nesting birds up close. Watch out for fulmars gliding just above the waves and patrolling the cliff edges, and gannets diving from spectacular heights and bombing into the sea like missiles.

Bird colonies

Sea birds spend most of the year on the oceans, but in early spring they fly to coasts to breed on cliffs. They gather in vast colonies to build their nests and raise their young. A colony can have several thousand squawking seabirds crammed together into every available space – making one of the most dramatic sights of the seashore.

These puffins are nesting together on top of a cliff.

Birds to spot

Puffin
30cm/12"
Plump and colourful seabird, with a bright multi-coloured bill and bright red feet. Nests on the top of cliffs. April to August.

Rock dove
33cm/13"
Lives in cliffs. Ancestor of town pigeon. Dark blue and grey with red and green markings on neck. All year round.

Kittiwake
38cm/15"
Pretty, medium sized gull with yellow bill, grey legs and black tipped wings. Distinctive call that goes "kitti-waak". February to August.

Razorbill
41cm/16"
Black upperparts and white chest, with a thick, black bill. Lays eggs in crevices in cliffs. March to July.

Guillemot
42cm/16.5"
Dark brown upperparts and white chest. Some have a white eye ring. Lays a single, pear-shaped egg on a bare rock ledge. March to August.

Fulmar
47cm/18.5"
Plump, heavy bird with broad grey wings held out stiffly like a glider. White head with black eye ring. All year round.

Shag
78cm/31"
Deep green with a tufted crest on its head in the breeding season. Fast, direct flight. All year round.

Cormorant
92cm/36"
Can be seen stretching out its wings to dry. Dives underwater for fish. Also seen on rivers. All year round.

Gannet
92cm/36"
Pale yellow head, long neck and large wings with black wing tips. Looks white from a distance. Dives deep underwater to catch fish. January to September.

This fish is called
a shanny. It can be
found around rocky
shores.

In the sea

If you wade through shallow water or put on a snorkelling mask, you can find some of the most curious seashore creatures. From the clown-faced tompot blenny to the pipefish that looks like a shoelace, seashore fish have unusual appearances and even more unusual lives.

Cuckoo wrasse, for example, are pale, pink fish that all start life as females. But, after a year, some develop brilliant blue and yellow stripes – and turn into males. Sticklebacks are small fish that make underwater nests out of seaweed, and sea scorpions can change from red to green in a second, disappearing into their surroundings, so they can creep up on other fish, and lurch forward to swallow their prey in a single gulp.

WEEDY NESTS

Sticklebacks are unusual fish, as they make underwater nests. The male builds the nest out of seaweed and algae, binding it together with sticky threads that come out of his kidneys. Then he attracts as many females as possible by showing off his nest, and shaking his body up and down.

Watching fish

Fish are tricky to spot, as they like to stay hidden. They swim out to sea at low tide, only to return when the tide rises. The best place to start looking is in shallow water on a beach that's sheltered from the wind. The more weedy and sheltered the shore, the more fish will live there.

To find a fish, listen for a splash or a ripple that will give it away. Then, if the fish are small enough, dip a jar into the water to see if you can scoop one up and get a closer look – or use an underwater viewer (see p27).

Grey mullets swim in large shoals near the surface.

Lesser sand eels swim along sandy shores.

Sticklebacks can often be found among weeds.

This plaice is hiding in the sand.

This clingfish uses the sucker on its belly to stick itself to a rock.

When to look

The best time to spot fish is in the spring, when many fish are mating. Some fish, such as blennies, gobies and pipefish, spend the winter out at sea, and come to damp, weedy hiding places on the shore around March and April.

Spring is also the only time you'll get to see a lumpsucker, a huge, strange looking fish which can attach itself to rocks by a sucker under its chin. Between February and May, female lumpsuckers lay their eggs on rocky ledges near the shore, and the male stays with the eggs until they hatch.

This worm pipefish is hiding among brown seaweed.

Rock gobies can sometimes be found in rock pools.

A lumpsucker can use the sucker on its chin to stick itself to rocks.

JARRING

One way to see fish up close is to go 'jarring'. For this you'll need a long piece of string, a screw-top jar and some bait - such as scraps of cheese.

1. Tie the string tightly around the neck of the jar so it doesn't slip off. Fill the jar with water and place the bait inside.

Tie round twice and knot both sides

2. Lower the jar into some shallow water where you can see lots of small fish - and wait.

3. Once fish have entered the jar, simply pull it as quickly as you can to the surface.

4. Once you've looked at the fish, return them to where they came from.

Flatfish are brilliant
at disguising
themselves in the
sand. They look as if
they're lying on their
bellies, but they're
actually lying on
their sides.
When it's born, a
flatfish has eyes
on either sides of
its head. But, as it
grows, one eye moves
around the head until
both are on the same
side. Flatfish can
also change colour
to match the exact
shade of the seabed
underneath them.

Hide and seek

When you spot a fish, it will be easier
to identify if you know the names of its
different parts. These names are used in field
guides and can be useful for taking notes.

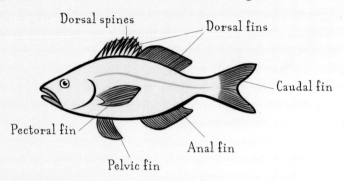

Dorsal spines

Dorsal fins

Caudal fin

Pectoral fin

Anal fin

Pelvic fin

Some fish can be especially tricky to see,
as they have markings that match their
background. This is called camouflage. The
long spined sea scorpion, for example, can
change colour from blue to green in a flash,
so it blends perfectly into its environment.

This long spined sea
scorpion has turned
pink and brown
to blend with
the pebbles
below it.

Fish to spot

Long spined sea scorpion
Up to 18cm/7"
Has venomous spines on its back. Hides in seaweed in rock pools. Is often dark brown and cream, but can change colour.

Sand eel
Up to 20cm/8"
Thin and long with a pointed jaw. Yellowish green with blue, silvery tints. Can burrow up to 50cm (20") into the sand if alarmed.

Dab
Up to 25cm/10"
Brown with darker blotches. Feeds on sea urchins, fish, worms, crustaceans and molluscs.

Corkwing wrasse
15-25 cm/6-10"
Found in shallow water and rock pools in the lower zone. Females are greenish brown, males are more brightly coloured.

Butterfish
25cm/10"
Found under rocks, among seaweed and stones on all kinds of shore. Lays eggs in winter.

Plaice
25-40cm/10-16"
Eyes on the right hand upper side, which is dark brown, with orange spots. Usually found on sandy shores.

Flounder
Up to 50cm/20"
Varies from brown to greyish green. Oval shape, with both eyes on the right hand side of the head.

Ballan wrasse
Up to 60cm/23"
Found in rock pools and on weedy shores. Young fish is green, older fish are more reddish brown, with small white spots all over.

Thick-lipped grey mullet
Up to 70cm/28"
Dark greenish or blue grey, with a white belly. Seen in large shoals near the surface.

Snorkelling

If you can swim well, you could put on a
mask, snorkel and fins, and disappear into
a silent, underwater world. Snorkelling can
be a great way to see animals and plants in
their natural habitat.

If you're very lucky, you might even spot
a cuttlefish. These shy creatures are the
magicians of the undersea world. They can
change their colour, pattern and even the
texture of their skin in an instant, so they
can hide almost anywhere.

Creatures to spot

Shore clingfish
6.5cm/2.5"
Flattened, triangular
head. Clings to rocks
with sucker located just
behind its head. Green,
brown or red. Stony
areas and rocky crevices.

Montague's blenny
Up to 8cm/3"
Brown with pale blue
spots. Lives in rock pools,
and eats acorn barnacles.
Like all blennies, it does
not have scales.

Sand goby
Up to 9cm/3.5"
Small, sandy coloured goby. Dark spots on the first dorsal fin, blotches along the sides. Found in shoals in shallow water.

Lesser weever
Up to 14cm/5.5"
Buries itself in the sand in shallow water. Has venomous spines. Feeds on shrimps and crabs as well as small fish.

Sand smelt
15cm/6"
Found in large shoals near the surface of the water. Pale, silvery yellow, with a dark stripe on one side.

Shore rockling
15-25cm/6-10"
Long, brown fish, found in rock pools and under stones and seaweed on rocky shores. Uses its barbels to find food.

Sea stickleback
Up to 15cm/10"
Long thin fish, with a pointed snout and sharp teeth. Very fierce, may attack fish larger than itself.

Tompot blenny
30cm/12"
Lives on rocky shores in pools and shallow water, under stones or among seaweed. Lays its eggs under flat stones.

Common cuttlefish
Up to 30cm/12"
Found near sandy and muddy shores. Can change colour very quickly when frightened.

Lumpsucker
Up to 50cm/20"
Blue, greyish or greenish. Male has a red belly in the breeding season. Uses sucker under chin to cling onto rocks. Rocky shores.

Common octopus
Up to 1.3m/51"
Has stout tentacles and warty body. Can change colour. Found on sea floor or in rock pools.

Jellyfish

If you go swimming or snorkelling, you
might well see a jellyfish floating by. Made
up of 97% water, with no brain, heart or gills,
jellyfish are pretty simple creatures. But they
move in the same way as space rockets – by
jet propulsion. They suck water up into their
bodies and then eject it, which sends them
shooting in the opposite direction.

Sea gooseberry
1cm/0.5"
Transparent, shimmering
oval body, the size of a
small gooseberry. Has
two long, sticky tentacles
which it uses to catch
prey. Harmless.

By-the-wind-sailor
3cm/1"
Floats at sea, but
sometimes washed ashore
in huge shoals. Has a thin
fin on its float, which
directs which way
it drifts. Harmless.

Aequorea
Up to 15cm/6"
Floats in the sea, but is
sometimes washed up on
shore in the summer.
Harmless.

Portuguese
man-o-war
15cm/6"
Each animal is actually
made up of lots of tiny
creatures, which live,
breed and move together.
Is sometimes
washed onto
the shore.
Stings.

Moon jellyfish
Up to 25cm/10"
Almost transparent
body, with four
horseshoe shaped tissues
underneath. Harmless.

Lion's mane jellyfish
Up to 50cm/20"
Tentacles, covered with
stinging cells,
can be up to
3m/10ft
long.
Harmless
to humans.

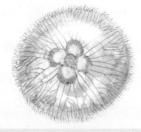

Spectacular slugs

With their bright colours, sea slugs look like land slugs in fancy dress. But their appearance isn't just for show – it's a brilliant disguise, because sea slugs look just like what they eat.

A sea slug that grazes on an orange sponge is orange. A sea slug that munches on a blue anemone is blue. The slug blends in, so it's less likely to be seen – and eaten.

SHORE WARS

One amazing feature of sea slugs is how they defend themselves. Many sea slugs are able to eat poisonous sponges, absorb the poison and then use it to repel predators. They can also eat jellyfish and absorb their stinging cells. They can then sting anything that attacks them.

Green sea slug
3cm/1"
Lives on seaweed in the middle and lower zones, and in shallow water. Colour changes from green to red, depending on what it is eating.

Limacia clavigera
Up to 3cm/1"
Body usually white, with yellow or orange fronds along its back. Feeds on algae on the lower zone and in shallow water.

SEA HARE

One of the strangest seashore animals is a sea hare. It looks a lot like a sea slug, but it's actually a mollusc, and has a shell inside it. It can be as large as 20cm (8"), and is a purply brown colour. When it's attacked, it releases huge clouds of purple dye. Then it uses two wings on the sides of its body to swim away. Look out for sea hares on rocky shores in summer.

Sea lemon
Up to 6cm/2"
Very common. Found under stones on rocky shores, or in the shallow water. Feeds on sponges, particularly the breadcrumb sponge.

Grey sea slug
Up to 8cm/4"
Found on rocky shores under stones, in rock pools and in shallow water. Feeds on sea anemones, absorbing their stinging cells.

A bottlenosed dolphin
leaps out of the water.

Near the shore

If you stand on a cliff and look out to sea, you could spot some of the mammals that live there. You might see a seal, effortlessly bobbing along in the water – or, if you're very lucky, you could catch a glimpse of a porpoise or a dolphin.

The best way to see seals is to go to the beaches where they breed and have pups, while if you want to see dolphins, you could go on an organized boat trip. You might spend hours on the ocean, getting cold, wet and seasick, but it will be worth it to see a dolphin leaping out of the water. You might even see the shiny dark skin of a whale breaking the surface, blowing a giant spray of water into the air, and then sliding back down into the deep.

IDENTIFYING SEALS

There are two main types of seals in northern Europe: grey seals and common seals. The easiest way to tell them apart is by looking at their faces.

Grey seals have longer muzzles and parallel nostrils.

 Common seals are smaller than grey seals.

Watching seals

Seals spend most of their lives at sea, but when they come to the shore they are fantastic to watch. They gather in noisy groups of up to several thousand animals, all crooning and hooting as they lie on the shore, or slither off rocks into the sea.

If you watch seals lumbering along a beach, you might think they are pretty clumsy animals. But underwater, seals are swift and graceful.

They are brilliantly adapted for life under the waves. Their huge eyes let in lots of light, which allows them to see well underwater as well as on land. They can hear all the sounds of the undersea world, and communicate with clicking and trilling noises. They can dive down to 200m (700ft) or more, and their sensitive whiskers can detect even the tiniest movements of their prey.

A common harbour seal diving

Watching seals

The best way to see seals is to go to the shores where they breed or moult (shed their fur). During the breeding season, you could see males (called bulls) fighting for the best spot on the beach, while the females (called cows) stay in the water to mate with the bulls.

Two male seals fighting for territory

A year later, the cows return to the same shore to give birth. You might see mothers feeding their babies (called pups) and protecting them from predators, such as gulls.

Seals also come to shore to moult. It's several weeks before their new coat is ready for them to waddle down to the sea and slip into the ocean.

SEAL FEAST

Before they come to the shore to breed, male seals stock up on food. They can eat up to 5 kg (11 lbs) of fish in one meal - the equivalent of eating 44 hamburgers.

A mother keeps her pup close to her, to protect it from predators.

This seal is moulting. Its old fur falls off. Its new fur is underneath.

A group of bottlenosed dolphins leaps out of the water.

Dolphins and porpoises

A dolphin has a curved fin along its back.

A porpoise's fin is straight-edged and triangular.

Dolphins are the acrobats of the sea. They often travel in large groups, whistling and clicking as they jostle, dive and leap right out of the water. Porpoises look very similar to dolphins, but they are much shyer animals, and only come to the surface to breathe. The easiest way to tell dolphins and porpoises apart is by their differently shaped fins.

AH-AH-AH-AH-TSHOO!

When whales breathe out they create a cloud of spray above the water, called a 'blow'. A whale's blow looks a bit like a sneeze, which might have inspired this song by Flanders and Swann:

"I'm lost and alone in a frozen zone
And I'm almost frozen too,
A shivering, quivering bottle-nosed whale,
The bottle-nosed whale with the flu...
Ah-ah-ah-ah-Tshoo!"

Whales

Whales are mammals. Like all mammals, they breathe in oxygen, so they have to come to the surface to breathe. They also stick their heads out of the water to look around (called spyhopping), and they sometimes leap out of the sea and fall back in with a splash. This is called breaching.

Sea watching

You might think that whales and dolphins are exotic creatures – but there are plenty of these exciting mammals to see in northern Europe. You can either spot them by going on a boat trip, or you can look out for a glimpse of them from the top of a cliff.

To do this you'll need a good pair of binoculars, and it's best to go on a calm, clear day when the sea's surface is as flat as possible. Find a cliff that juts out into the sea – and just start watching. Here are some tips to help you spot some of the most magnificent creatures in the sea.

FAB FACT

Although dolphins and porpoises look different to whales, they are both actually a kind of small whale. More than 29 different types have been spotted in northern Europe.

1. Look out to sea, searching for anything that disturbs the surface of the water.

2. Alternate this with looking out to sea through binoculars for a few minutes.

3. If you think you see a whale or a dolphin, keep looking around that area. It may take a few minutes for the animal to resurface, and the mammal may have moved quite a long way underwater before it appears again.

TOP TIPS FOR CLIFF WATCHING

*Look for waves breaking or appearing to go the wrong way.

*Look around for dolphins swimming around the bows of boats.

*Look out for large flocks of seabirds, these are often seen in the company of porpoises and minke whales.

Basking sharks swallow about 2000 cubic metres of water each hour - that's as much water as there is in an Olympic swimming pool.

The stomach of a basking shark is as big as a bath, but its brain is the size of a sausage.

Shark skin may look smooth but it is covered in tiny spikes. It used to be used to make boot soles.

Basking sharks

Sharks have a reputation for being sleek killing machines with razor-sharp teeth. But actually, the most common shark in Europe is the basking shark, a gentle giant that only eats microscopic plants, called plankton.

Basking sharks certainly look like sea monsters. They are the second largest fish in the world. They can reach over 11m (35ft) in length – that's as long as a bus – and weigh up to 7000 kg (15,400 lbs) – as much as two elephants.

They feed by swimming along the surface of the water with their mouths wide open, filtering plankton from the water that passes through their mouths. They are sometimes seen close to the shore in the summer, when they come into bays to look for food and find partners for mating.

A basking shark swims along with its mouth wide open to draw in water.

Sea mammals and sharks to spot

Common seal
1.4-1.9m/4.6-6.2ft
Dark brown, tan or grey, with a lighter belly. Female is slightly smaller than male. Eats fish and sometimes squid. Can stay underwater for up to 30 minutes.

Harbour porpoise
Up to 1.6m/5ft
Blunt head and no beak. Small, triangular dorsal fin. Male is slightly smaller than female. Feeds on fish. Common.

Common dolphin
2-2.4m/6-7ft
Upper body is dark, lower yellow and tan. Short beak. Dark triangle under the dorsal fin. Male is slightly bigger than female.

Grey seal
2.1m/6.9ft
Colour varies from black with white spots to white with black spots. Male is much larger than female. Eats a variety of fish, squid and crabs. Pups have white fur.

White beaked dolphin
2.5-2.7m/8-9ft
Short, often white beak. Black back with a pale grey or white area behind the dorsal fin. Travels in large groups of up to 1,500 dolphins.

Bottlenosed dolphin
Up to 4m/13ft
Large head, short beak, often with a white tip on the lower jaw. Has a tall, sickle shaped dorsal fin. Acrobatic, often leaps out of the water.

Risso's dolphin
Up to 4m/13ft
Blunt, rounded head with no beak. Grey in colour, with white scars on the sides. Often seen breaching, spyhopping and tail slapping.

Minke whale
7-8.5m/22-27ft
Slender, triangular head. White band on its flipper. Frequently approaches boats. Sometimes seen with harbour porpoises and other whales.

Basking shark
Up to 11m/35ft
Light grey to black back. Stout body. Five long gill slits run from the head to the throat. Eats plankton. Summer.

Glossary

Here are some words in the book you might not know. Any word in *italics* is defined elsewhere in the glossary.

Algae Simple, rootless plants that grow in water.

Antennae A pair of feelers that extend from an animal's head.

Bi-valve A mollusc with two shells hinged together.

Camouflage Body markings which help an animal blend into its background.

Carapace The hard shell of a *crustacean*.

Crustaceans A large group of animals that have hard shells, jointed bodies and *antennae*.

Downwind In the same direction as the wind.

Driftwood Wood that has been washed onto a shore.

Estuary The place where a river meets the sea.

Field guide An animal and plant identification book.

Habitat A place where an animal or plant lives.

High tide The highest point that the water reaches on the shore.

Holdfast A structure anchoring seaweed to rocks and other hard surfaces.

Low tide The lowest point that the water reaches on the shore.

Lower zone *Zone* which is usually covered by the sea, except at very *low tides*.

Mermaid's purse A dogfish egg case.

Middle zone *Zone* which is covered and uncovered by the sea at every *tide*.

Mollusc An animal with a soft body, usually encased in a hard shell, for example, a limpet.

Neap tide The *tide* with the least variation in water level, occuring every two weeks.

Plankton Microscopic plants and animals that float along in the water.

Predator An animal that hunts other animals for food.

Saltmarsh A *habitat* in an *estuary* where salt tolerant plants live.

Species A type of plant or animal that breeds with others of its kind and can produce young.

Splash zone The highest *zone* on a beach, which is never covered by the sea.

Sand dune A ridge of wind-blown sand.

Scavenger An animal that eats the remains and waste of other animals.

Shingle Small pebbles on a beach.

Spring tide The *tide* with the most variation in water level, occuring every two weeks.

Strandline The line at the top of the beach where objects are washed up from the sea.

Test The skeleton of a sea urchin.

Tides The movement of the Earth's ocean surface caused by the gravitational forces of the Moon and the Sun.

Uni-valve A *mollusc* with one shell.

Upper zone *Zone* on a beach which can be left uncovered by the sea for days.

Webbed feet Feet which have a layer of skin stretched between the toes.

Wormcast A mass of sand or mud left on the surface by a burrowing worm.

Zones Different areas on a beach between the *high tide* and *low tide* marks.

Index

Acknowledgements

Every effort has been made to trace the copyright holders of material in this book. If any rights have been omitted, the publishers offer to rectify this in any subsequent editions following notification. The publishers are grateful to the following organizations and individuals for their permission to reproduce material
(t = top, m = middle, b = bottom, l = left, r = right):

Cover © **8t** © Iain Sarjeant / Oxford Scientific; **p1** © D. Hurst / Alamy; **p2-3** © Tom Uhlman / Alamy; **p4-5** © Botanica / Oxford Scientific; **p6-7** © P.J.Sharpe/Zefa/Corbis; **p10** (m) © FLPA / Alamy; **p12** (b) © David Chapman / Alamy; **p16** (b) © Linda Alstead / Alamy; **p17** (t) © Emma Lee/Life File/Photodisc/Getty Images; **p19** (b) © Paul Broadbent / Alamy, (m) © Stockbyte, (t) © Superstock / Alamy; **p22** (b) © Photothema; **p23** (m) tbkmedia.de / Alamy; **p24** © Christina Bollen / Alamy; **p28** (b) © NHPA/JEFF GOODMAN; **p30** (b) © Nature Picture Library / Alamy; **p32** (b) © Paul Kay / Oxford Scientific; **p34** (b) © Foto Natura Stock / FLPA; **p40-41** © Alan Howden - Uruguay Stock Photography / Alamy; **p49** (t) © Chris Windsor / Riser / Getty Images; **p 56-57** © PHILIP SMITH / Alamy; **p58** © Charles Stirling (Diving) / Alamy; **p62** (b) © Juniors Bildarchiv / Alamy; **p64-5** © www.ianbutlerphotography.co.uk; **p66** (b) © Andrew Darrington / Alamy; **p67** (tr)© www.ianbutlerphotography.co.uk; **p72** (b) © Pat Bennett / Alamy; **p74** (b) © Wolfgang Kaehler/CORBIS; **p76-77** © NHPA/GERRY CAMBRIDGE; **p80** (b) © Papilio / Alamy; **p82-3** © ANESTIS REKKAS / Alamy; **p86-87** © ImageState / Alamy; **p88** (b) © Norbert Wu / Minden Pictures / Getty Images; **p89** (t) © Les Gibbon / Alamy; **p90** 'The Whale (Mopy Dick)' from AT THE DROP OF A HAT by Flanders & Swann, 1957. By permission of the Estates of Michael Flanders & Donald Swann; **p91** (t) © blickwinkel / Alamy; **p92** (b) © Alan James / naturepl.com.

Additional designs by Laura Hammonds, Joanne Kirkby and Karen Tomlins
Cover design by Joanne Kirkby
Digital manipulation by Keith Furnival

Additional illustrations by John Barber, Ian Jackson, Kate Rimmer, Lizzie Barber, Trevor Boyer, Alan Harris, Annabel Milne, Peter Stebbing, David Baxter, Roland Berry, Hilary Burn, Terry Callcut, Victoria Gordon, Bob Hersey, Deborah King, Patricia Mynott, David Nash, Gill Platt, George Thompson, Peter Warner, Phil Weare and others.